بِسْمِ اللَّهِ الرَّحْمَٰنِ الرَّحِيمِ

THANK YOU

FOR PURCHASING THIS RAMADAN HIGH CONTRAST BABY BOOK

Thank you for choosing our High Contrast Ramadan Baby Book for your little one! We hope your baby enjoys the high contrast illustrations and designs. Your support means a lot to us and we would be grateful if you could take a moment to leave us a review. Your feedback will help other parents discover our baby book and improve our future creations.

★★★★★

Curious for more?
SCAN NOW

DON'T FORGET TO FOLLOW US ON AMAZON.COM

COPYRIGHT © 2023 BY

WayOfLife™
PUBLISHING

ALL RIGHTS RESERVED, NO PART OF THIS MY FIRST RAMADAN HIGH CONTRAST BABY BOOK MAY BE REPRODUCED IN ANY FORM WITHOUT WRITTEN PERMISSION FROM THE PUBLISHER

Why High Contrast Images?

Decades of research show that time spent looking at high contrast images is important for a baby's cognitive development. Until about the fifth month, babies use their eyes as the primary source for information about the world and how it works.

Once your baby's pupils are working and his two eyes start to coordinate, he'll be compelled to look at high contrast images, especially from birth to 14 weeks old.

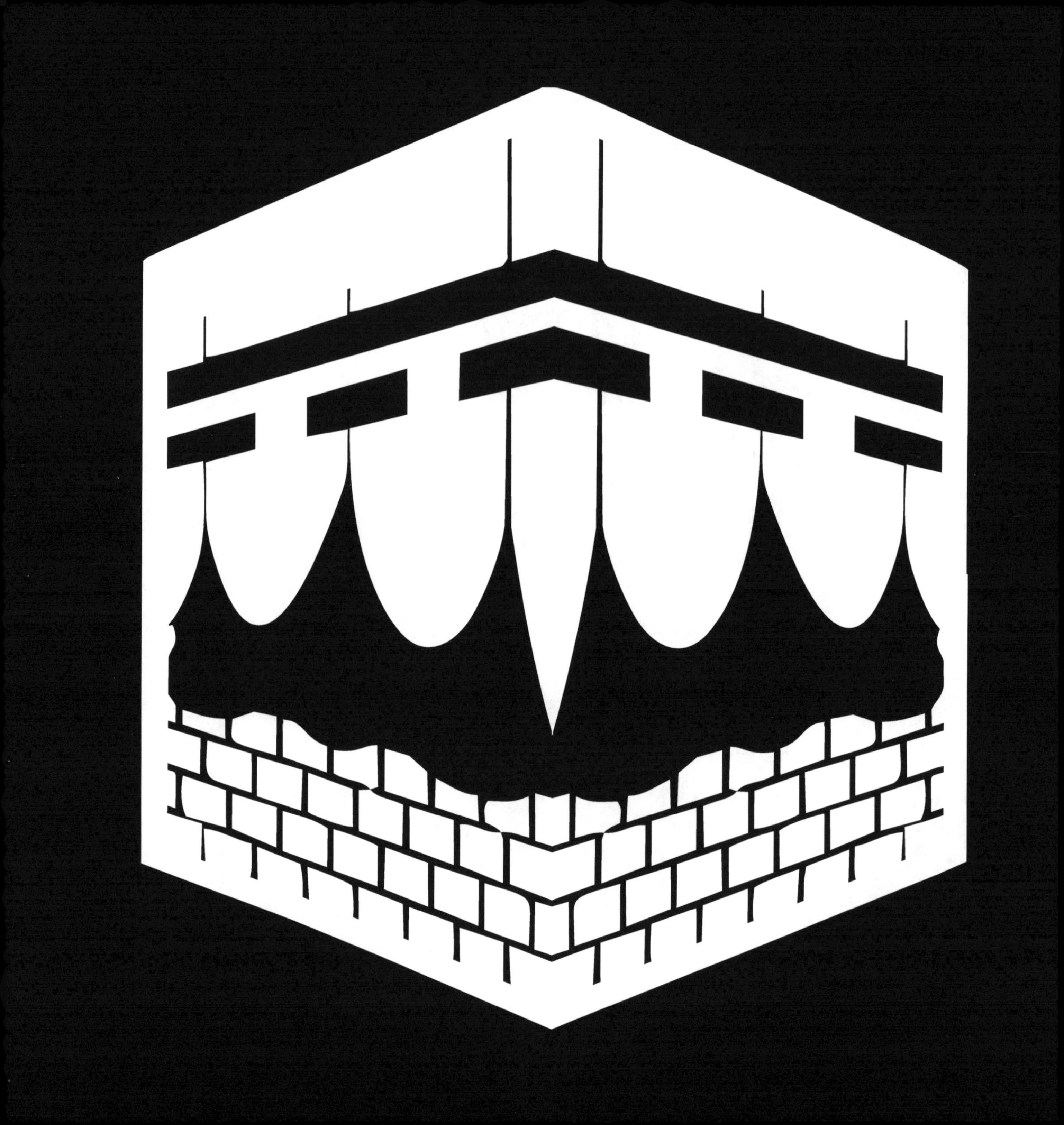

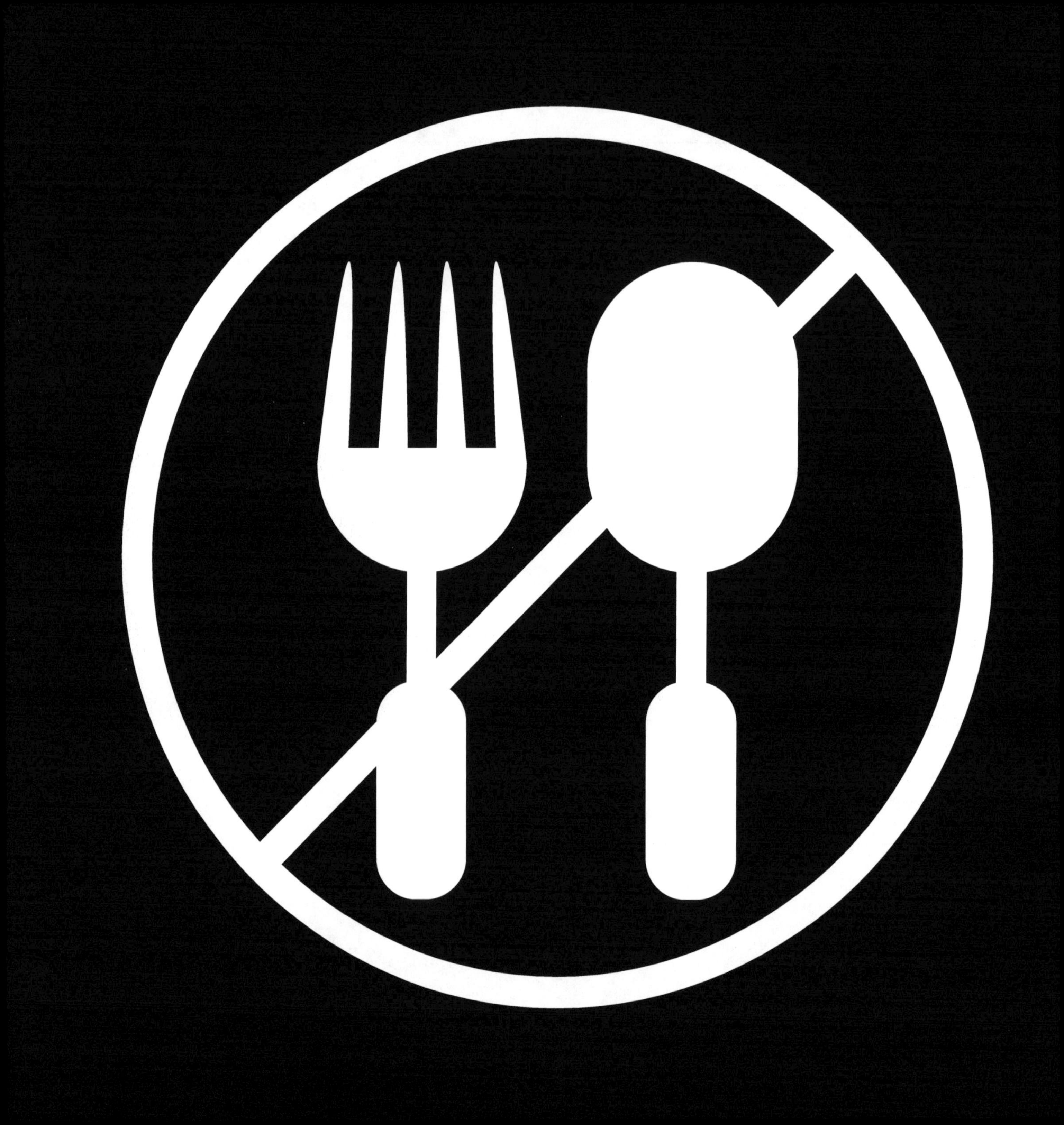

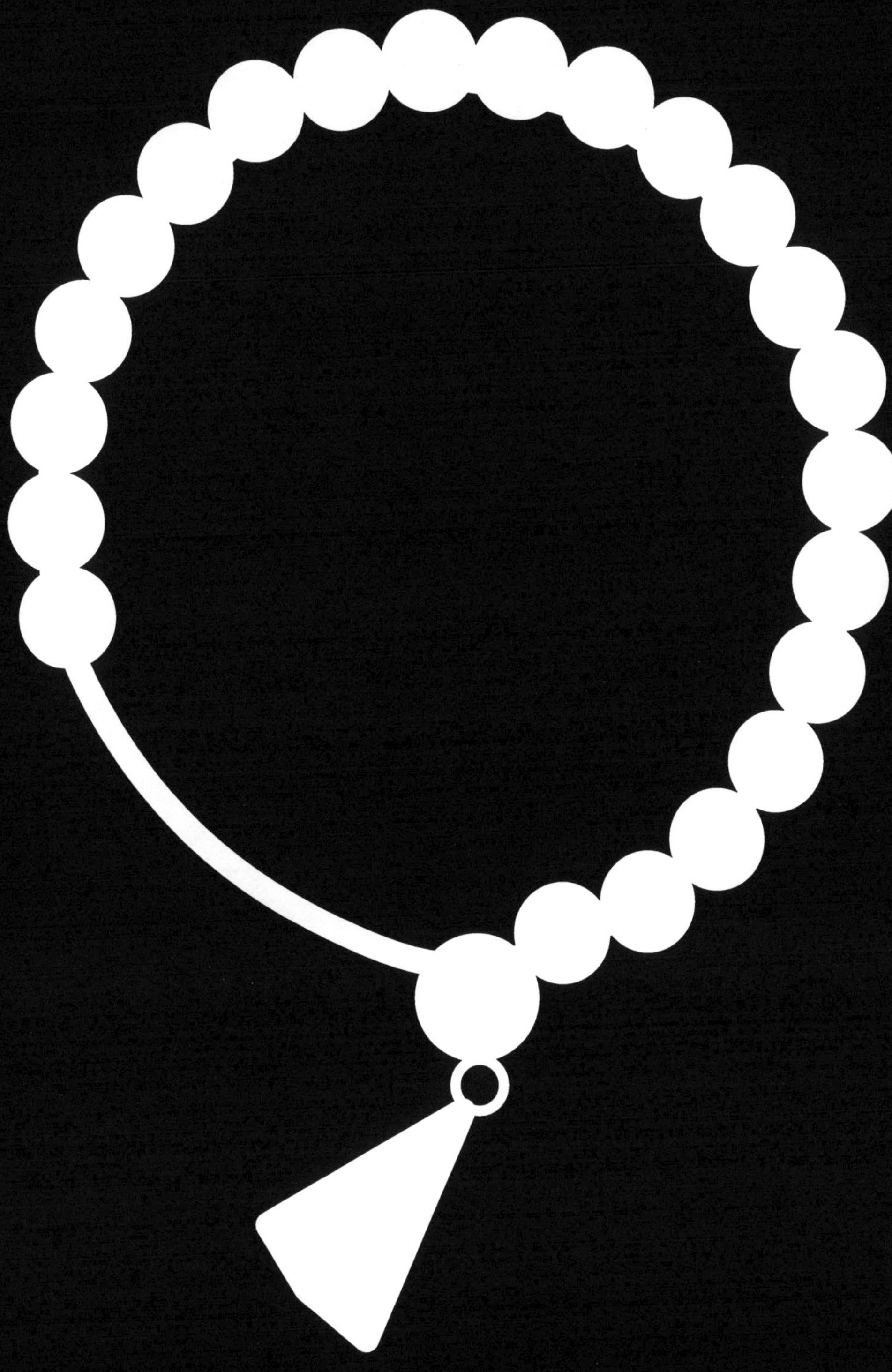

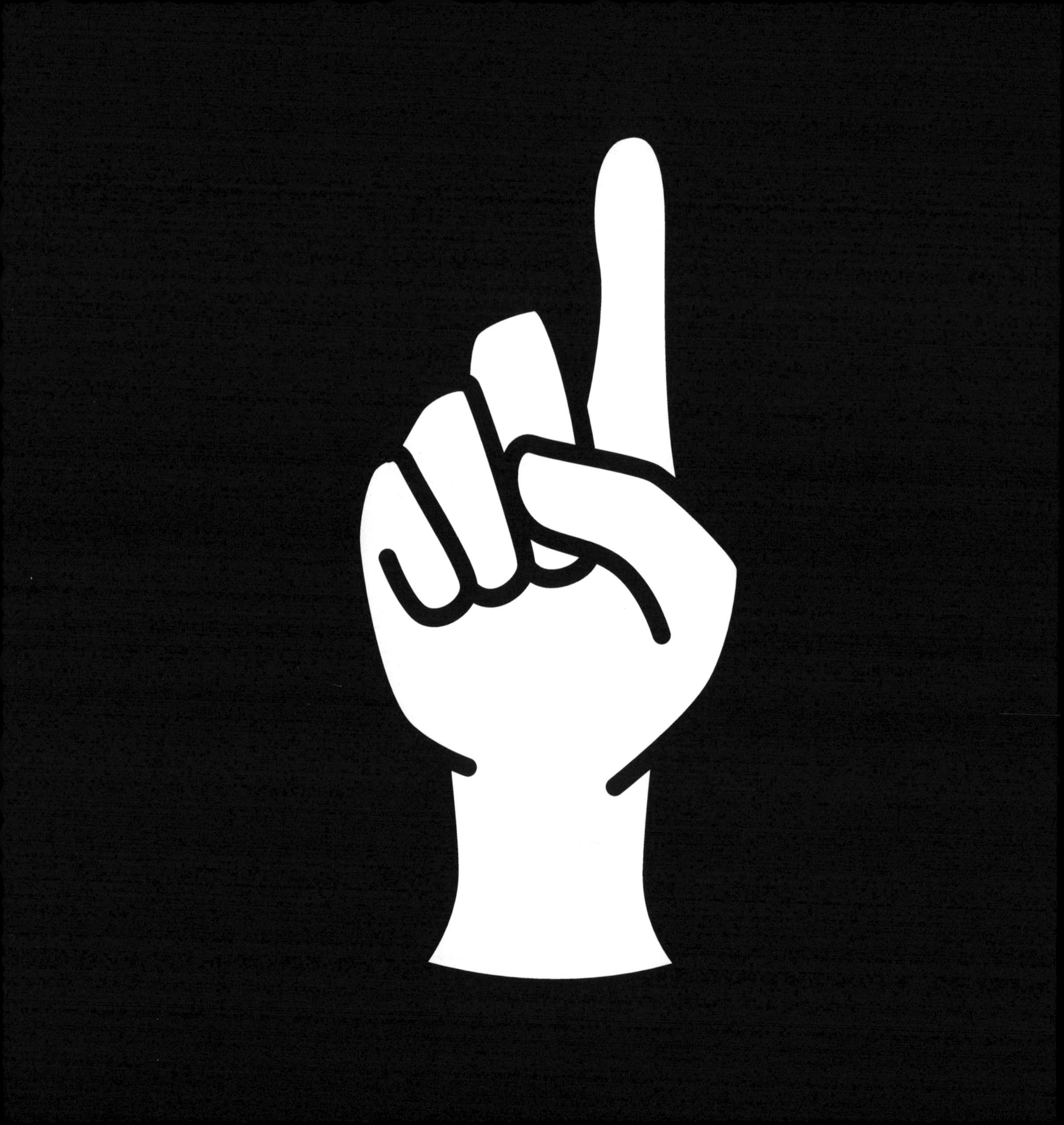

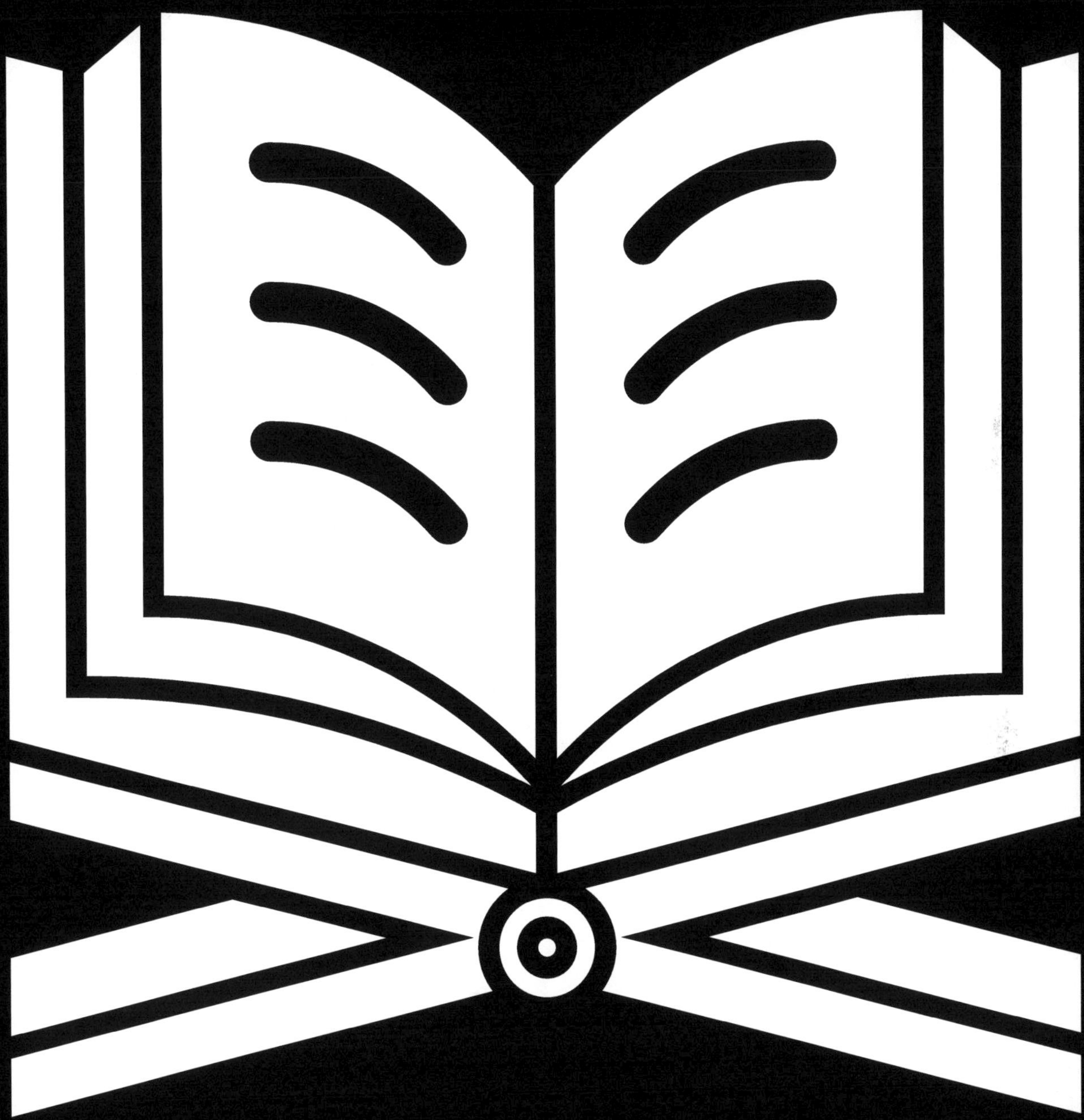

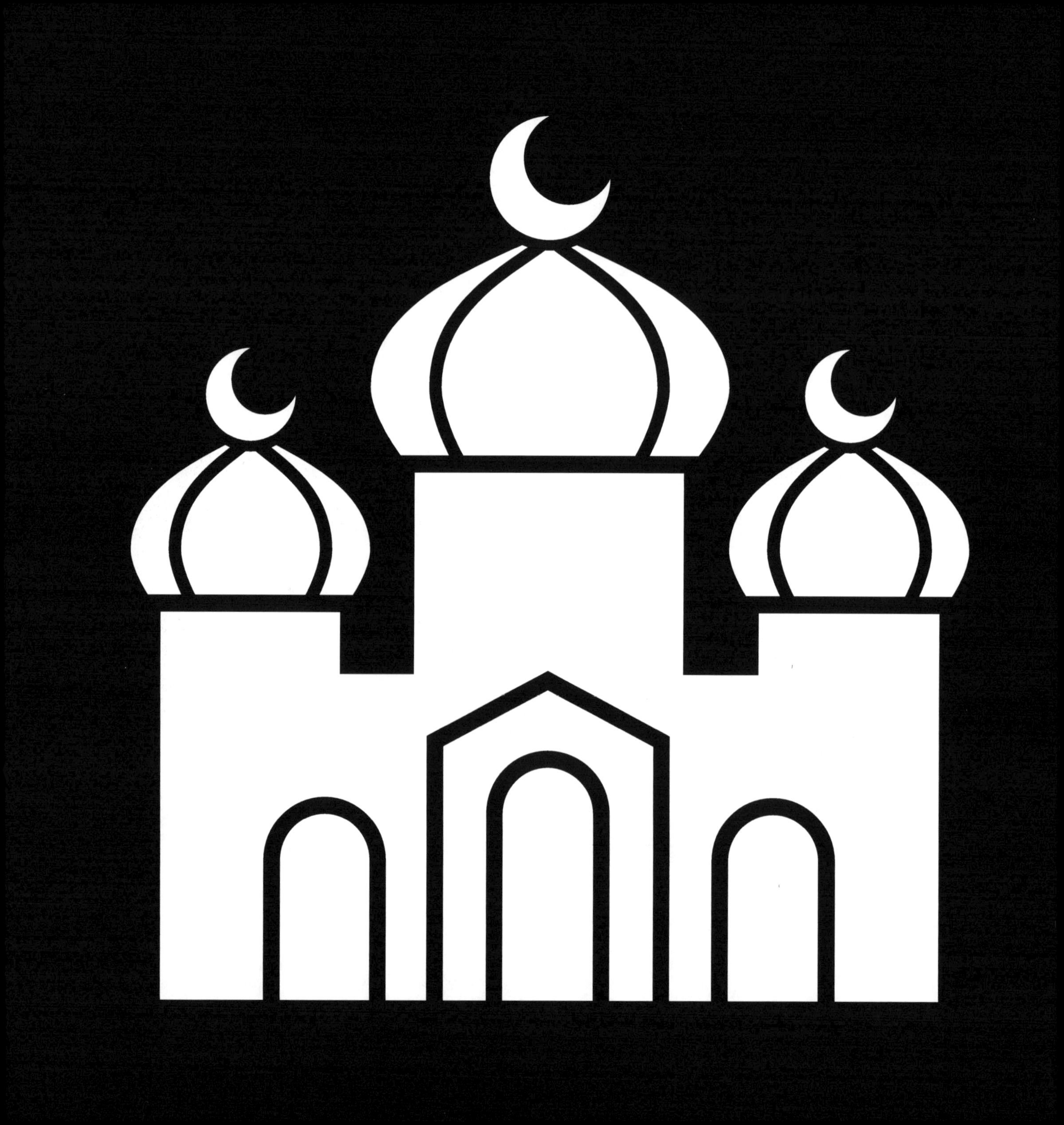

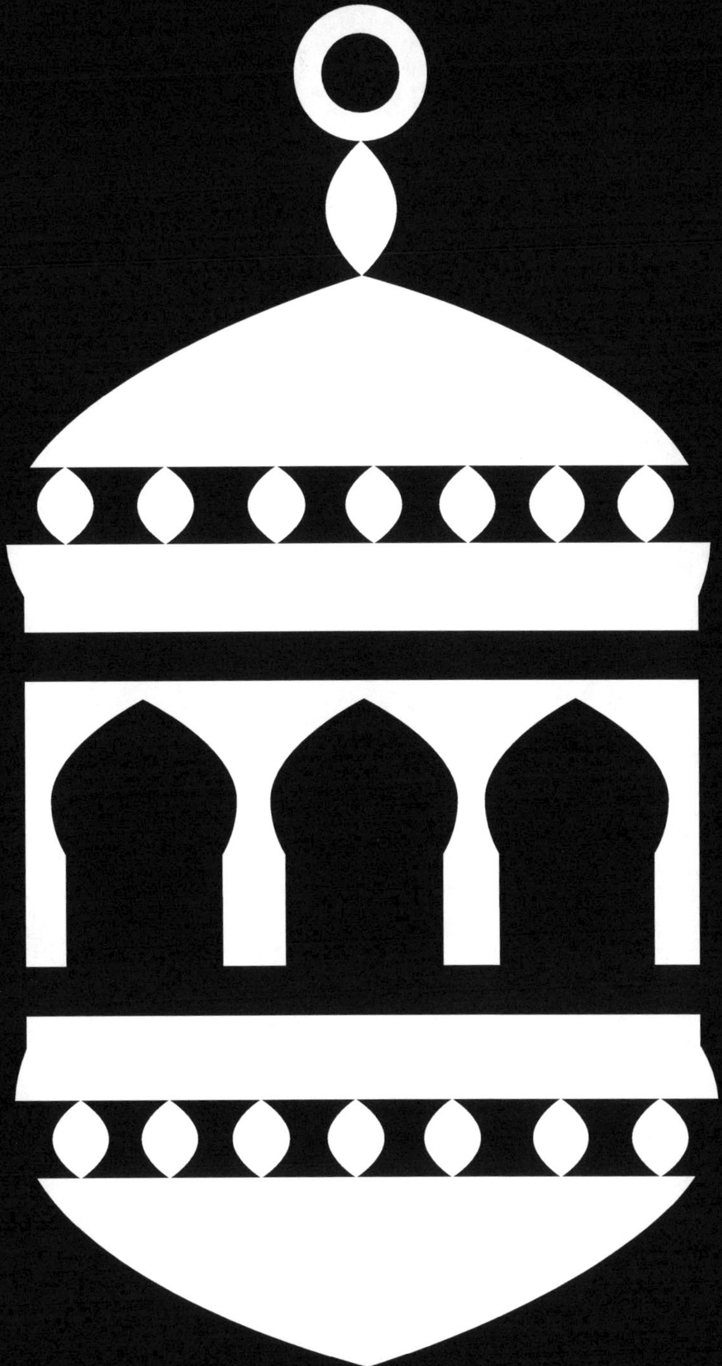

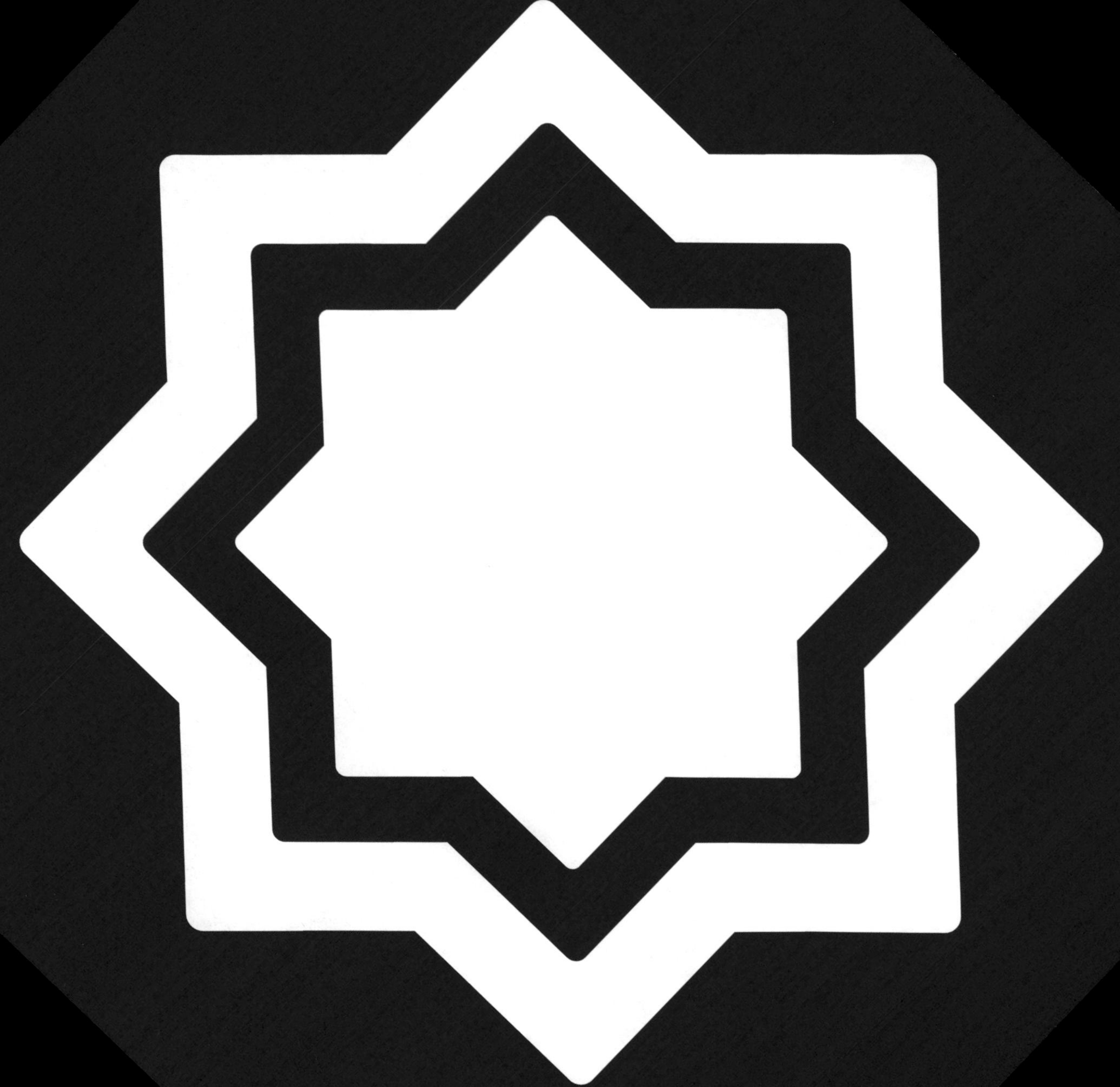

حلال

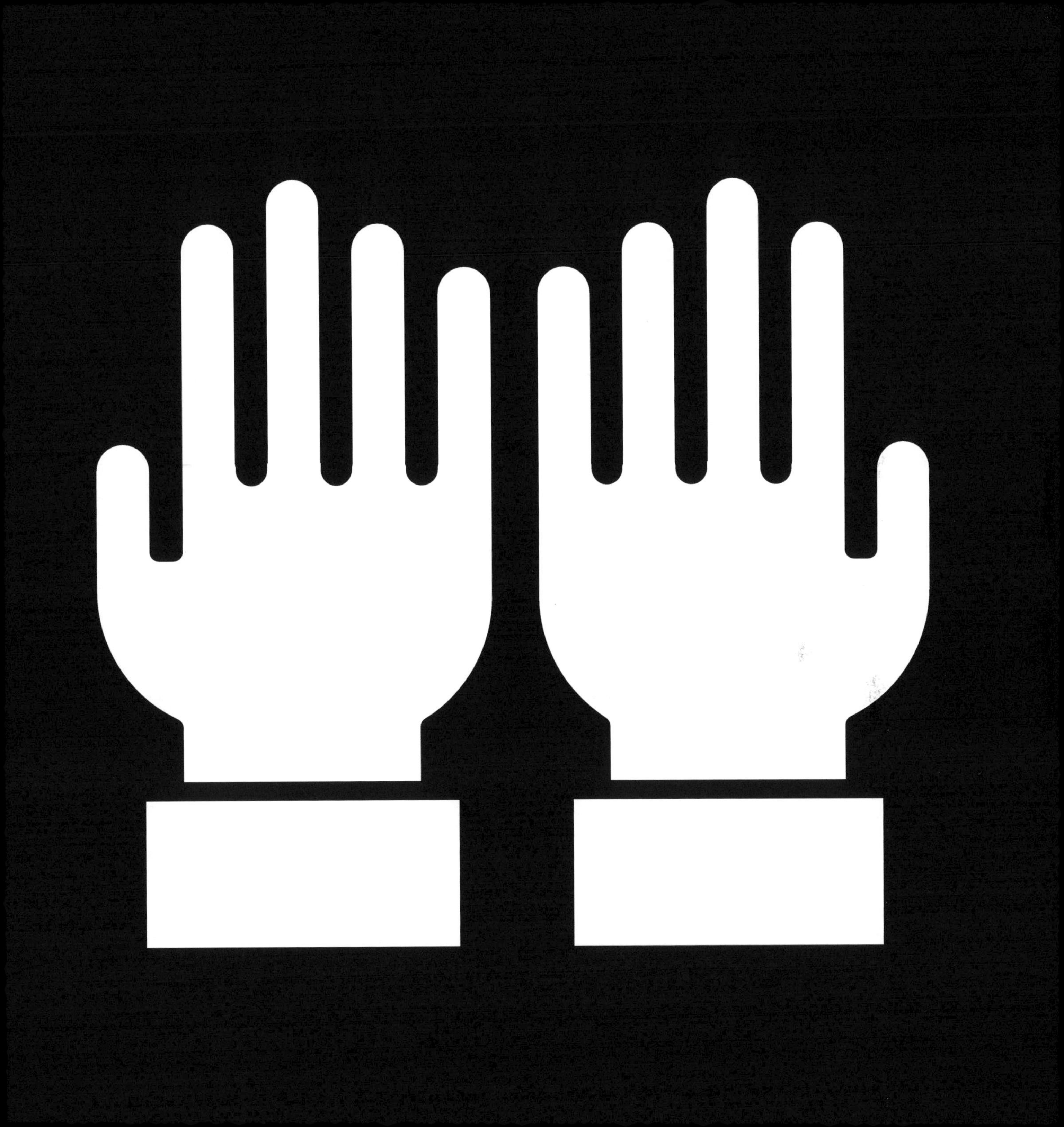

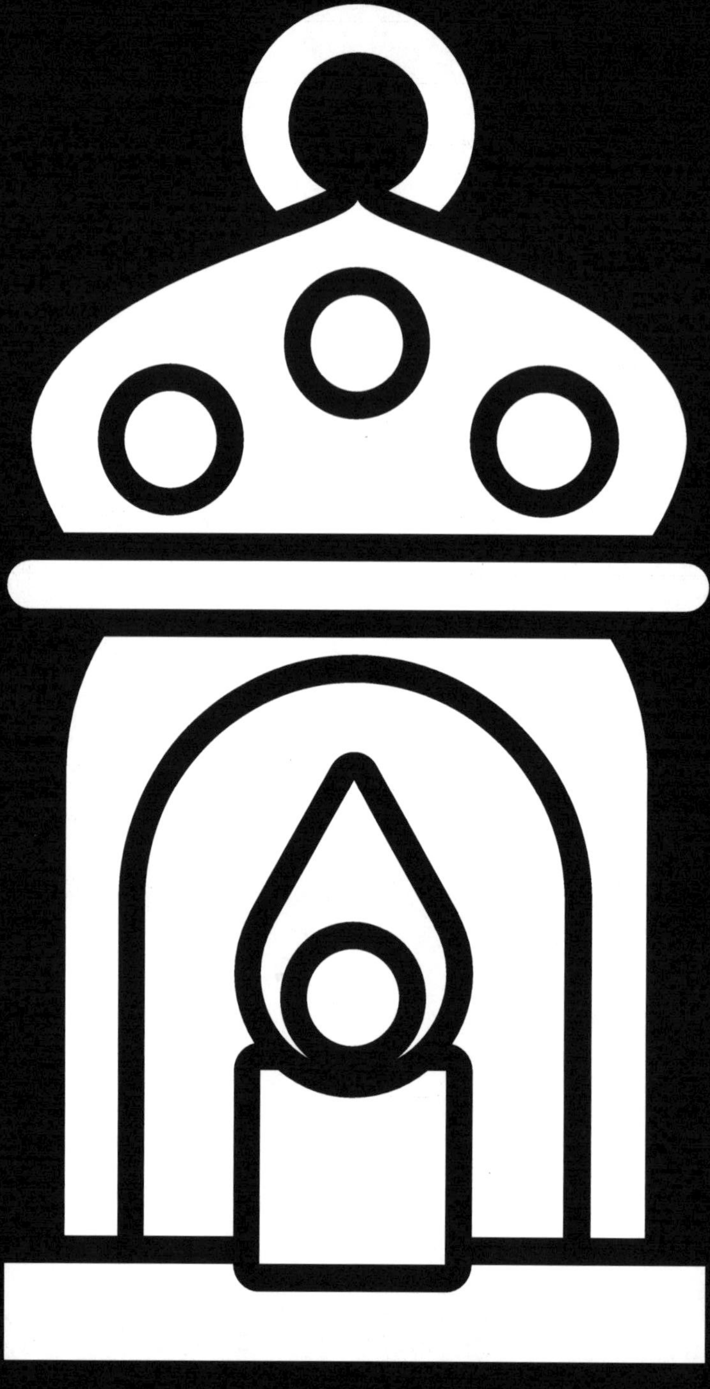

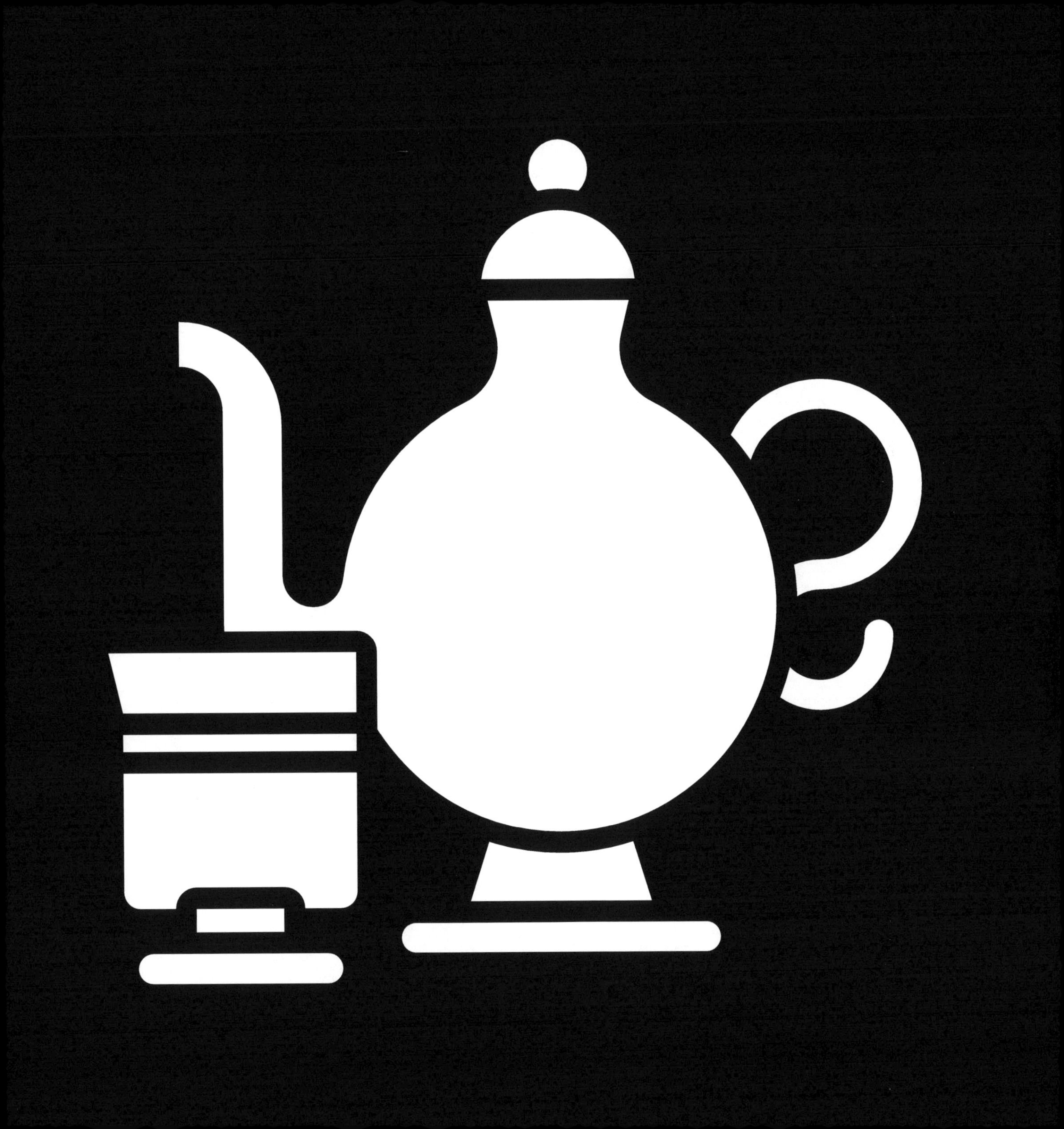

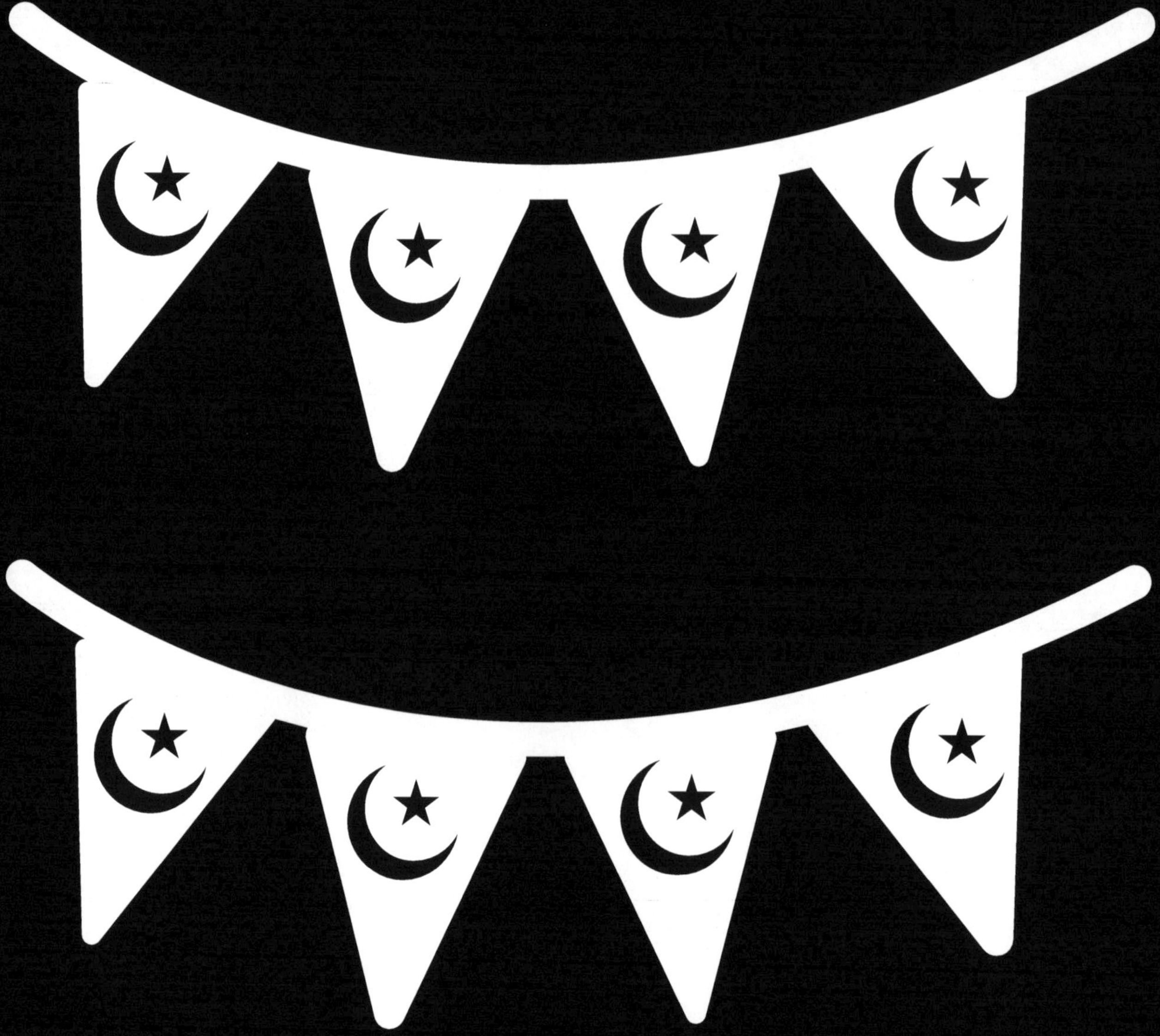

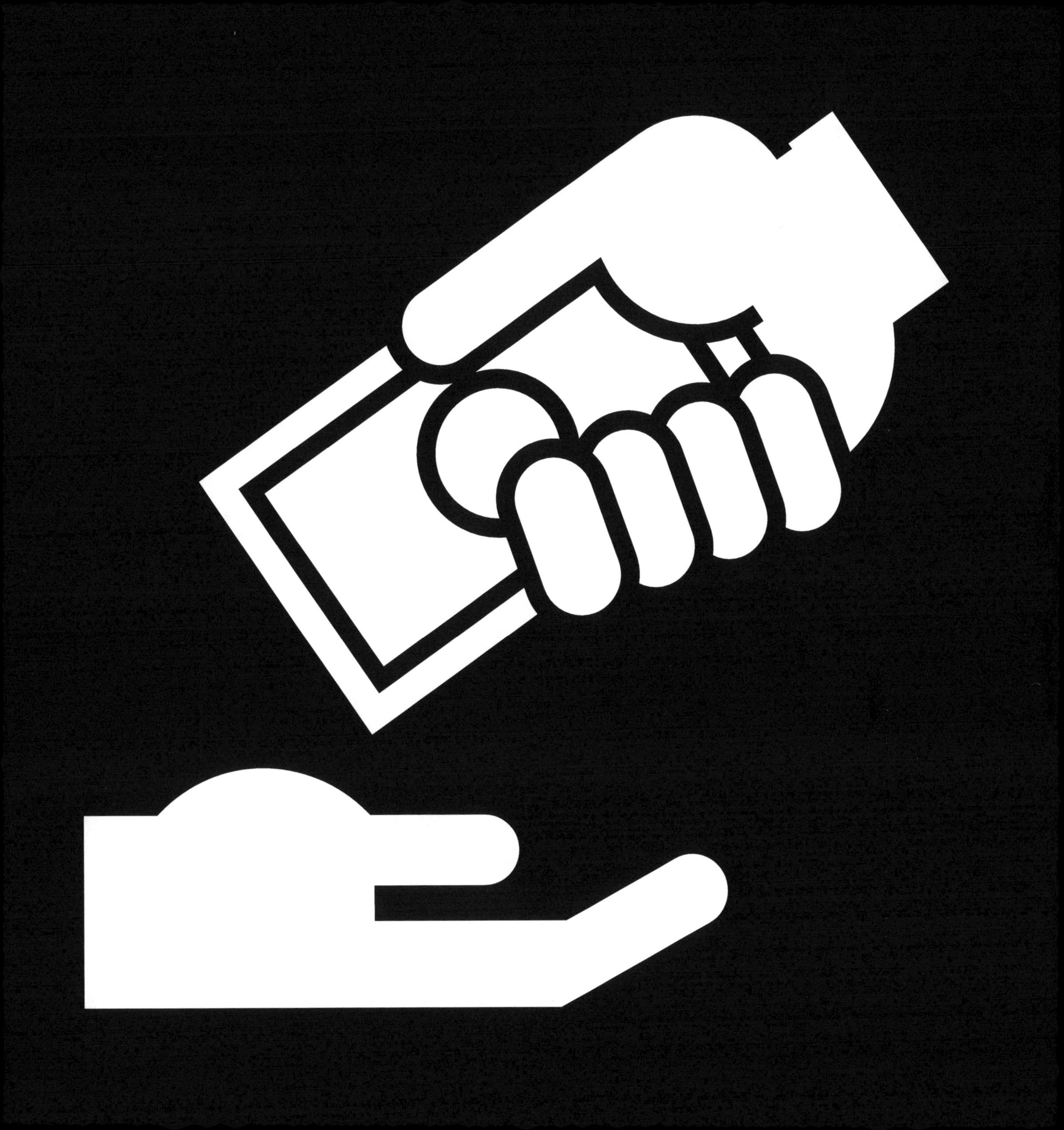

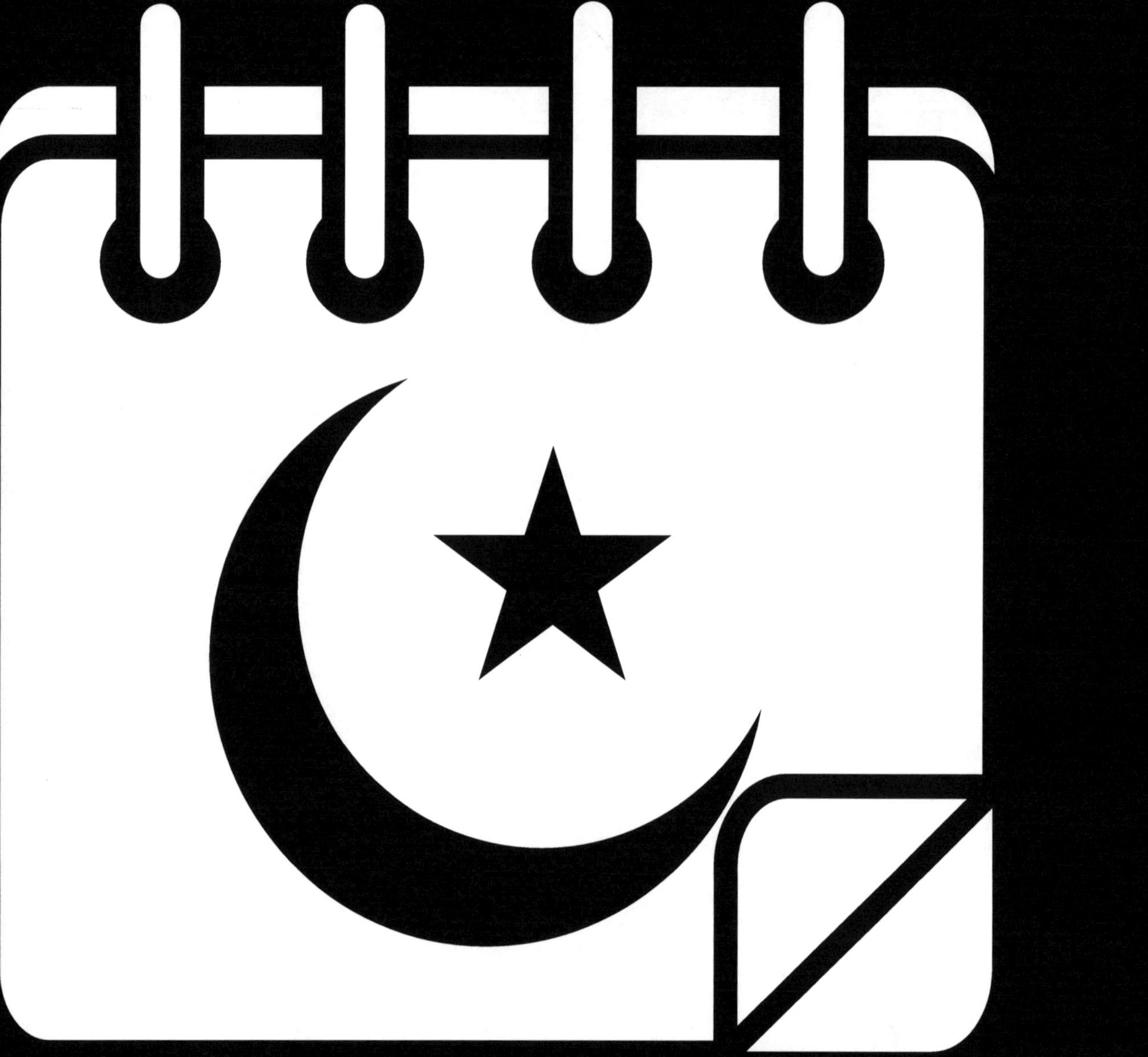

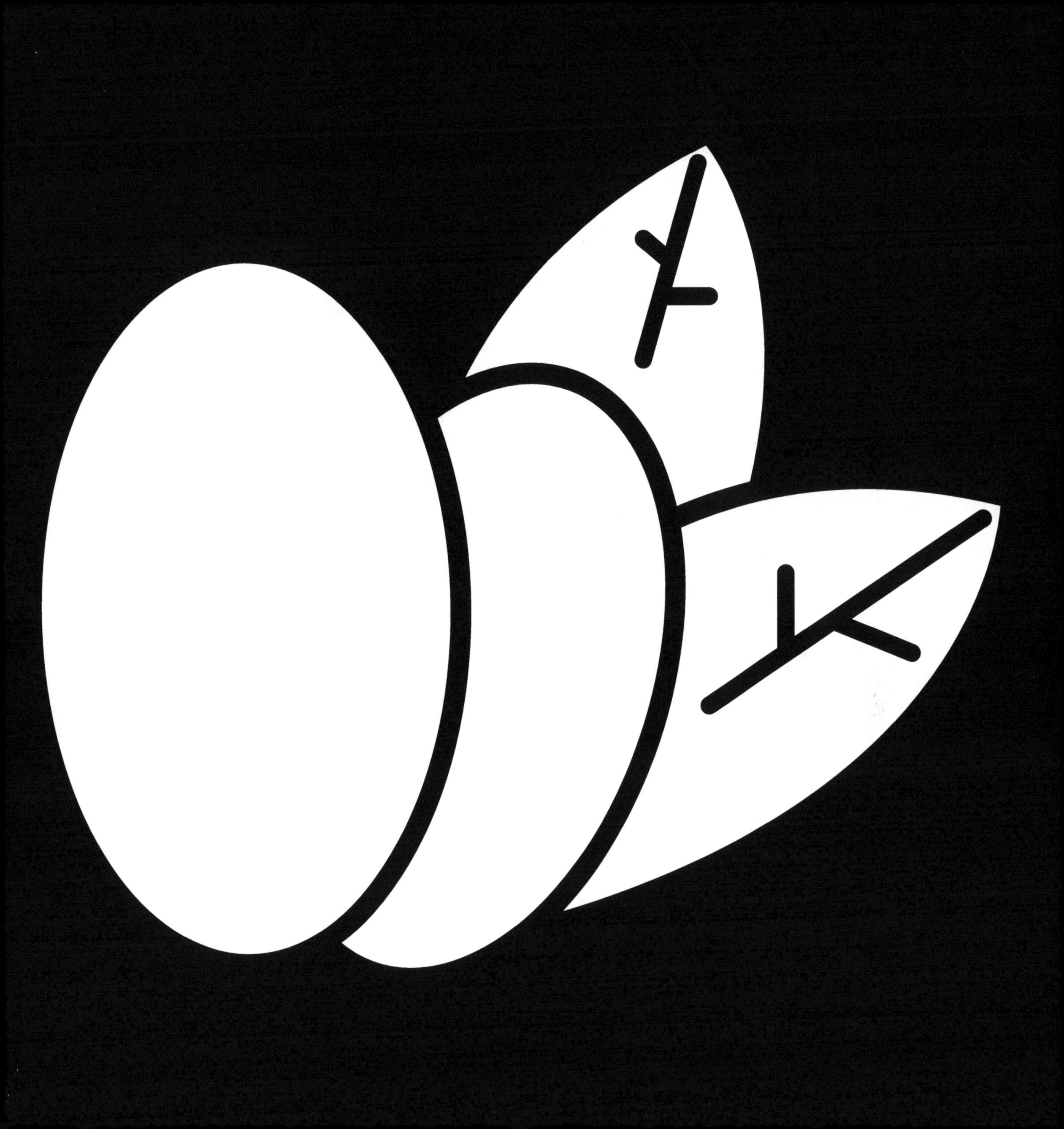

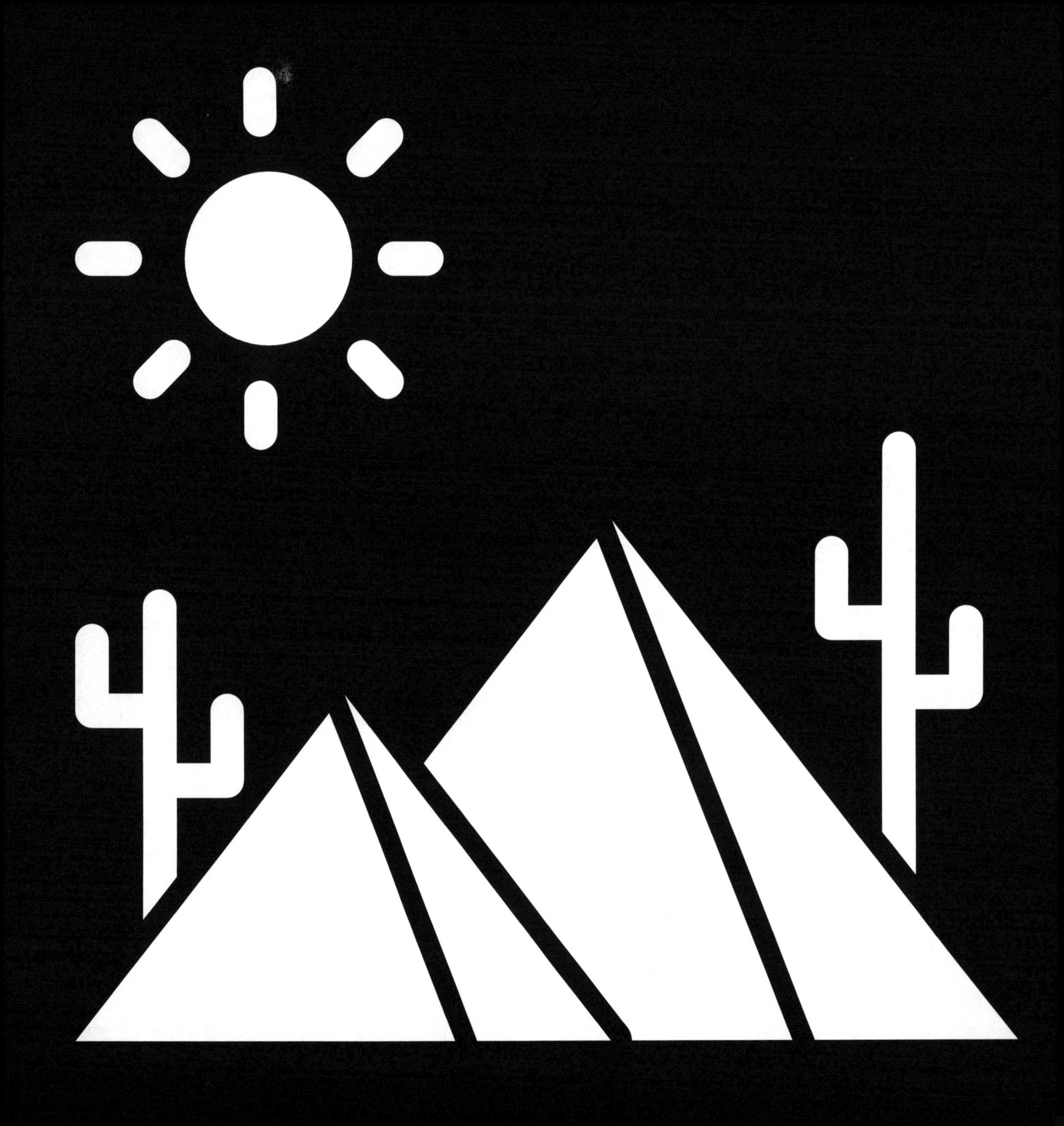

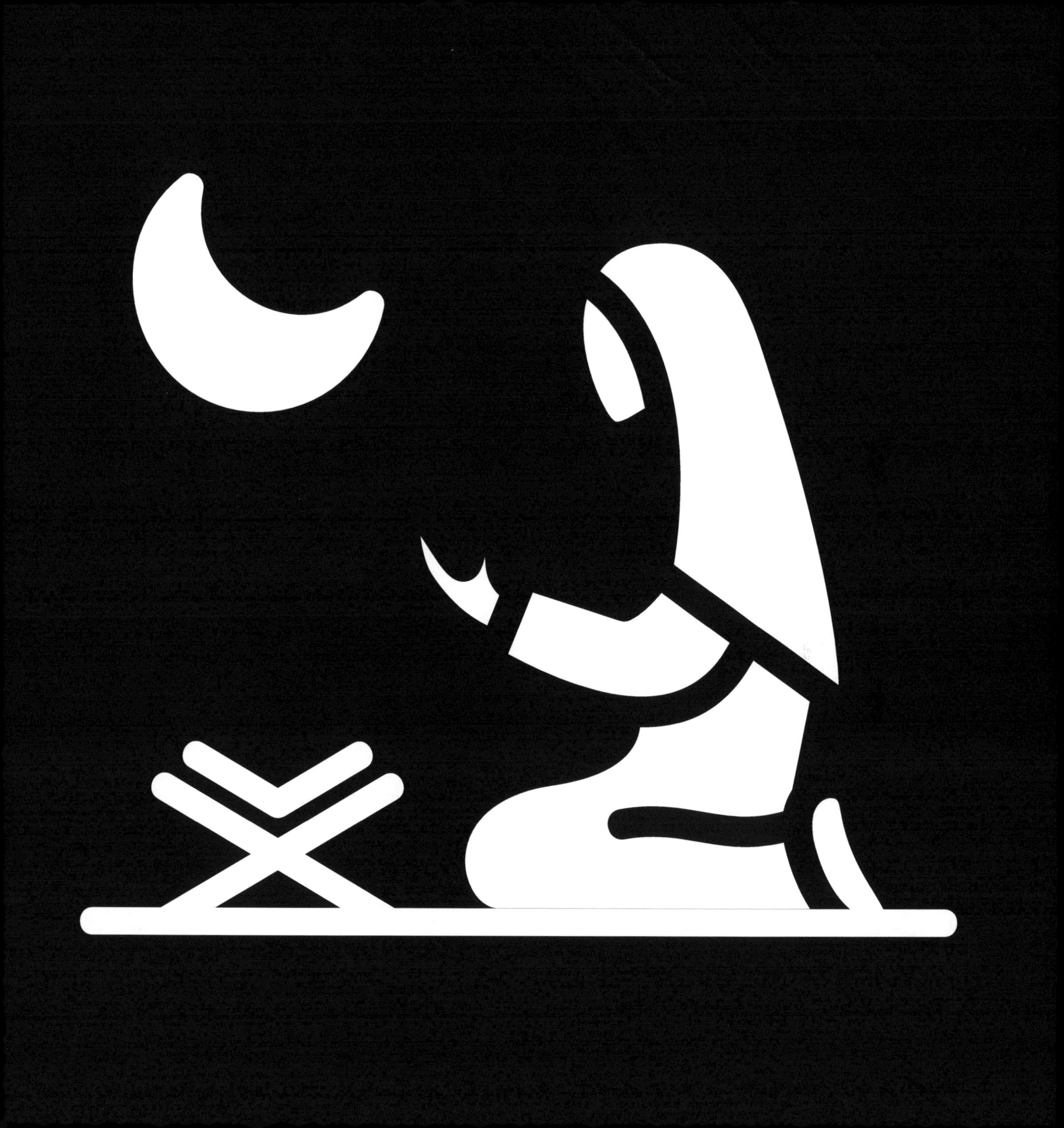

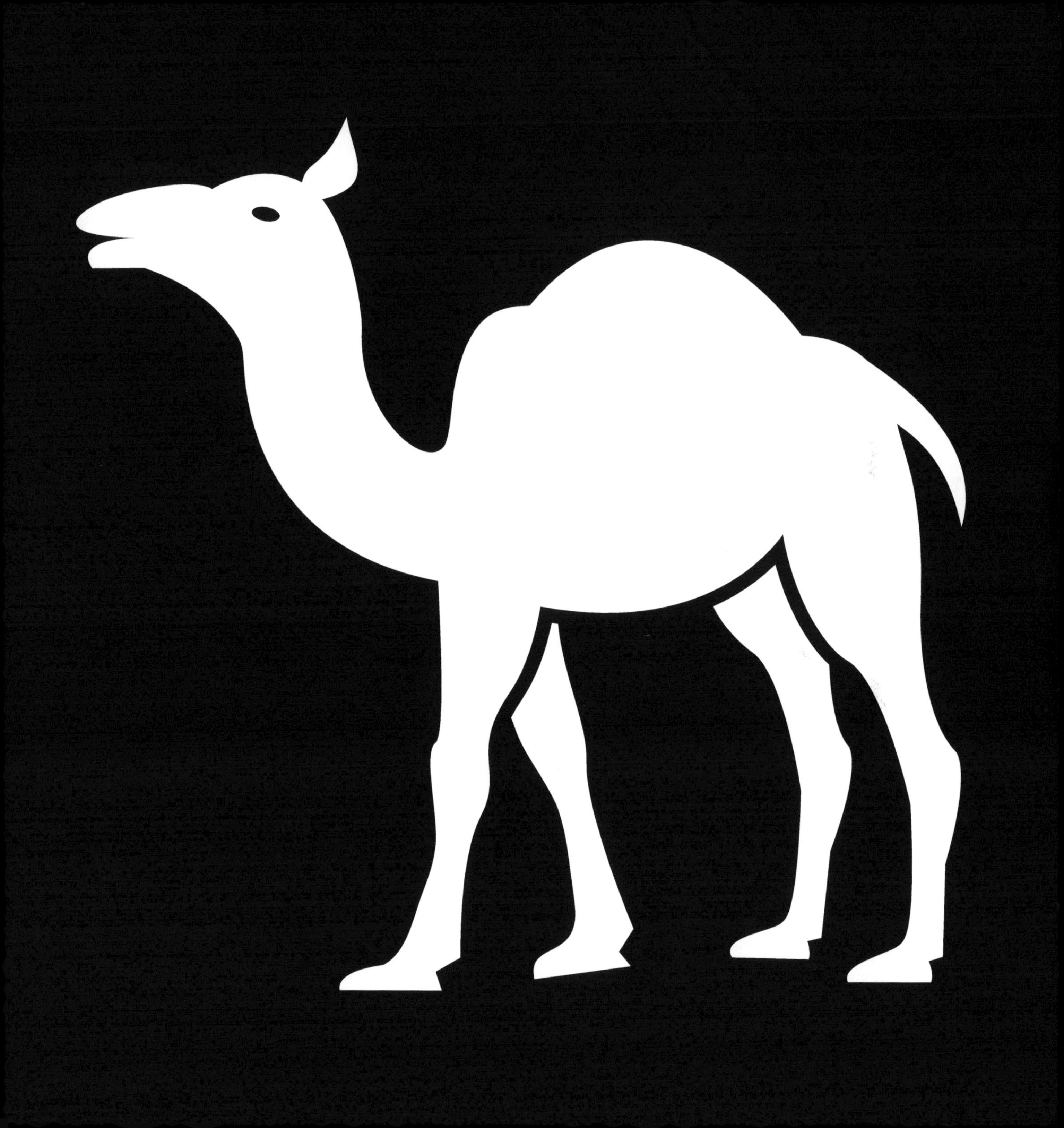

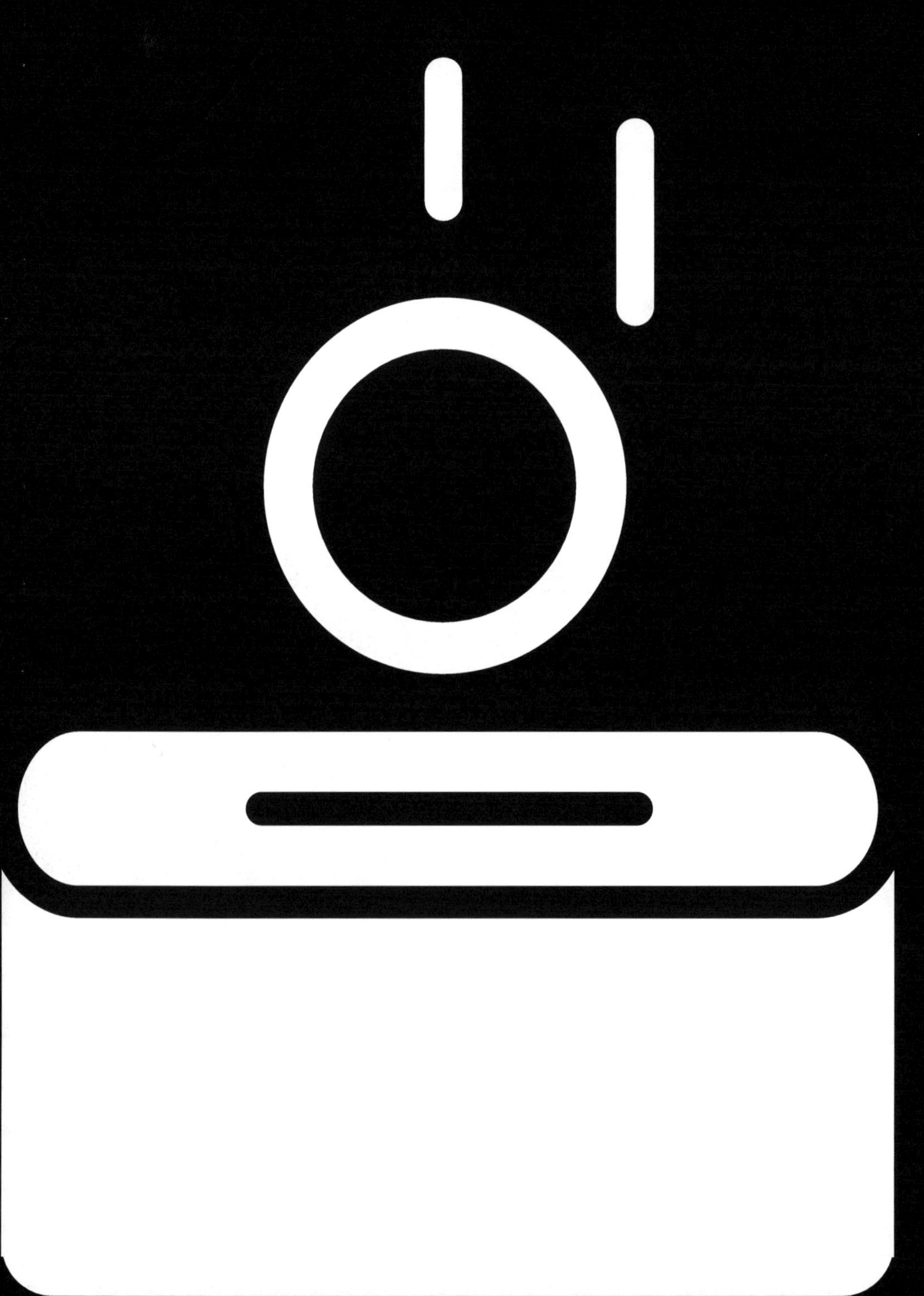

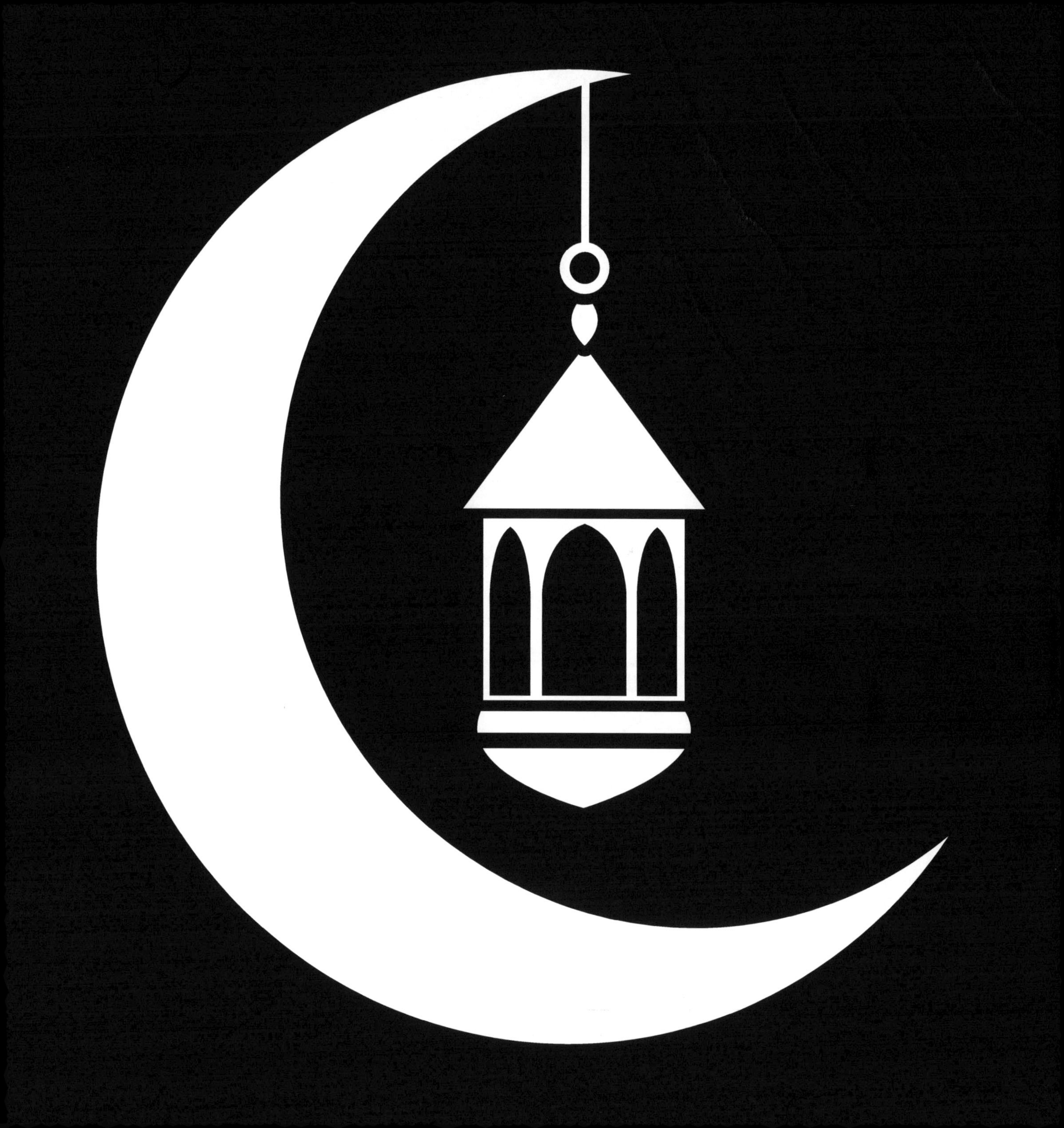

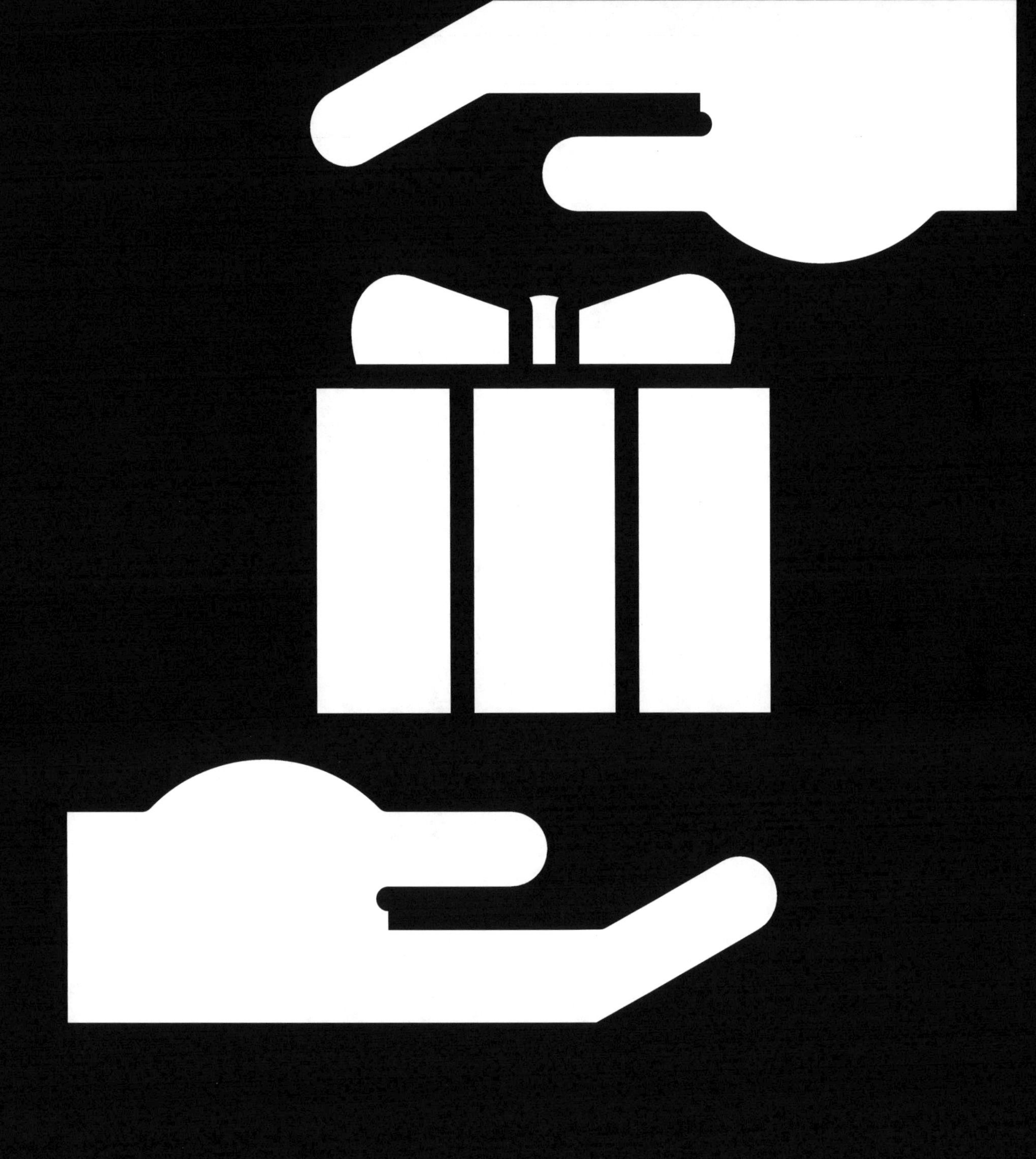

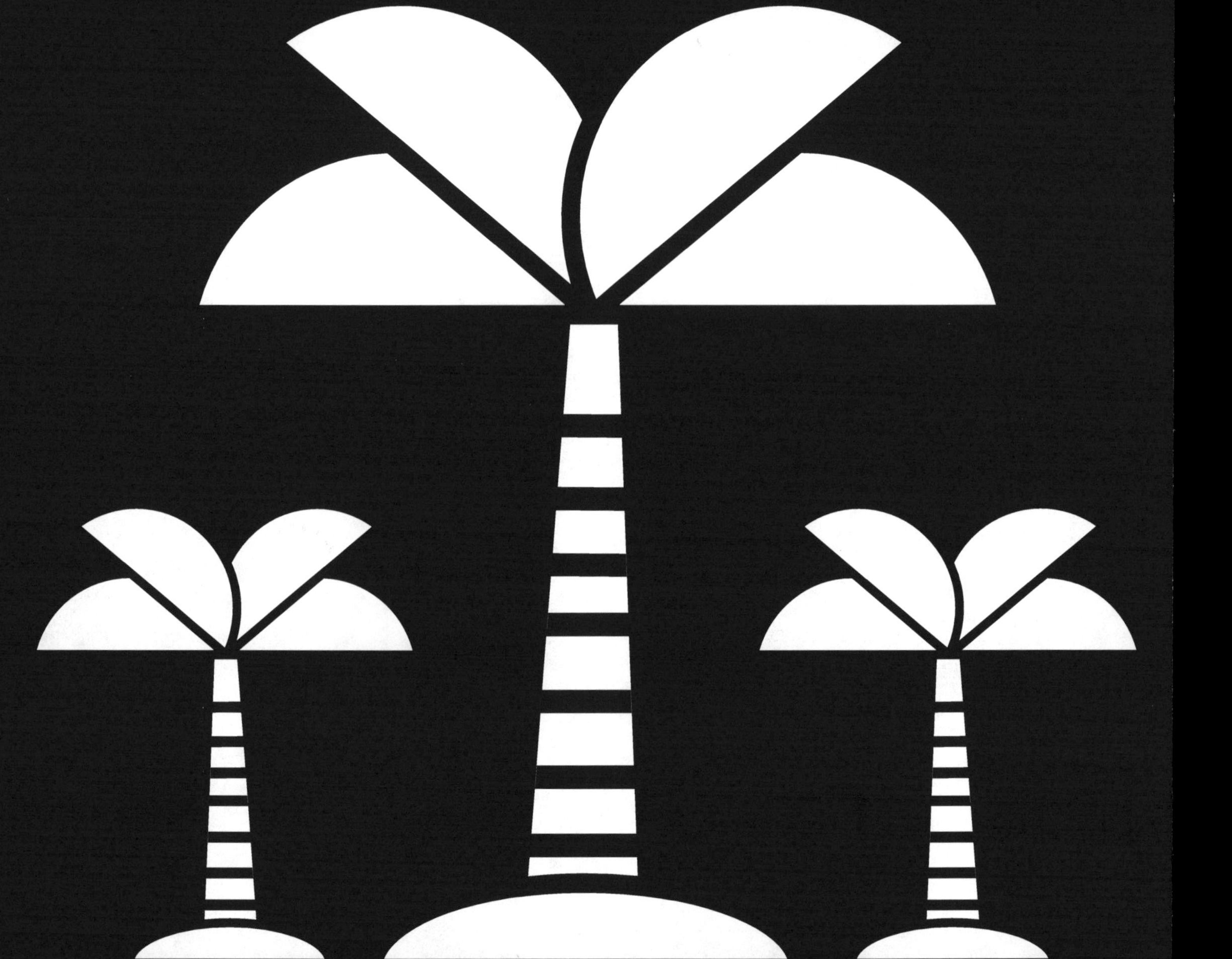

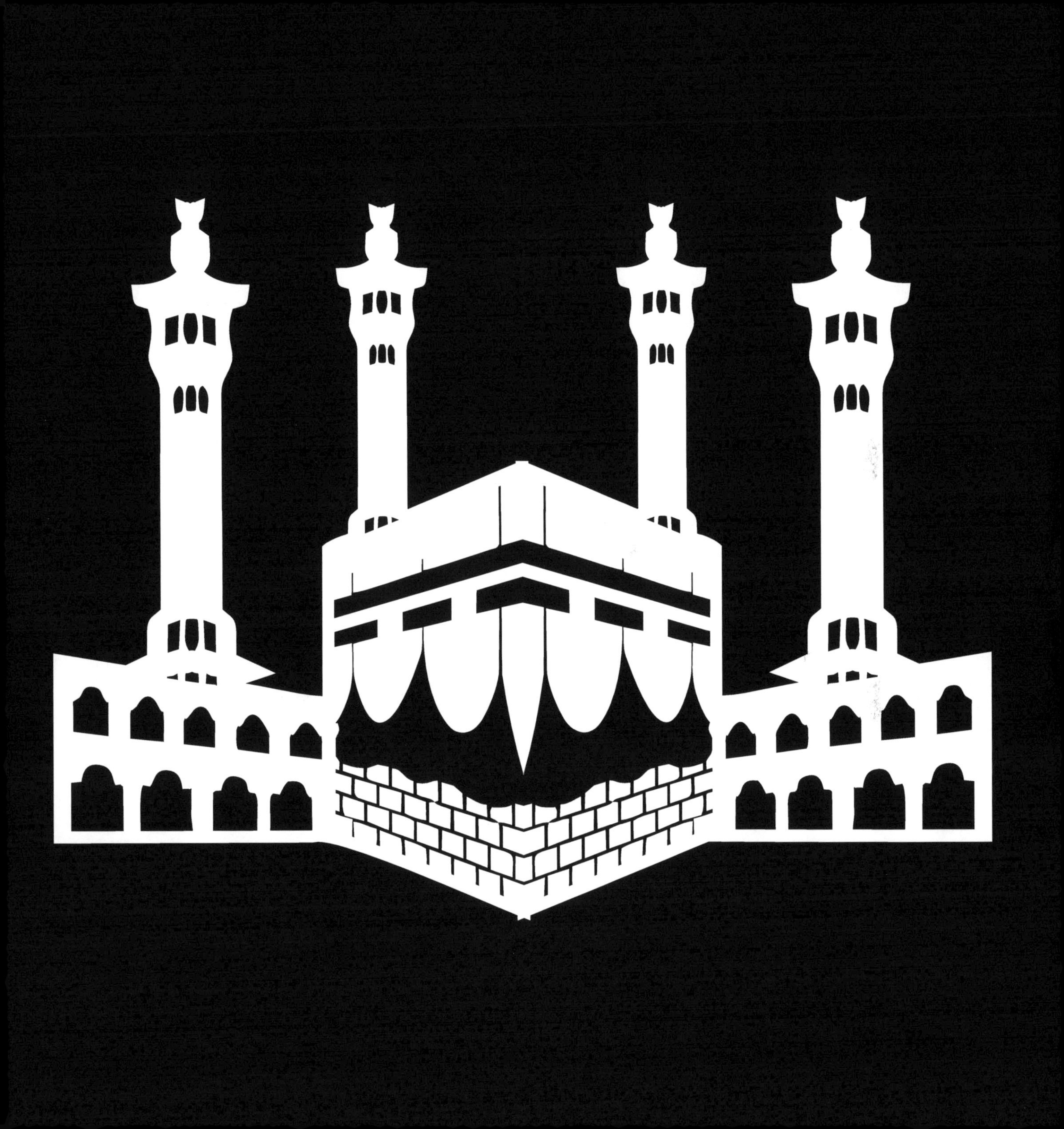

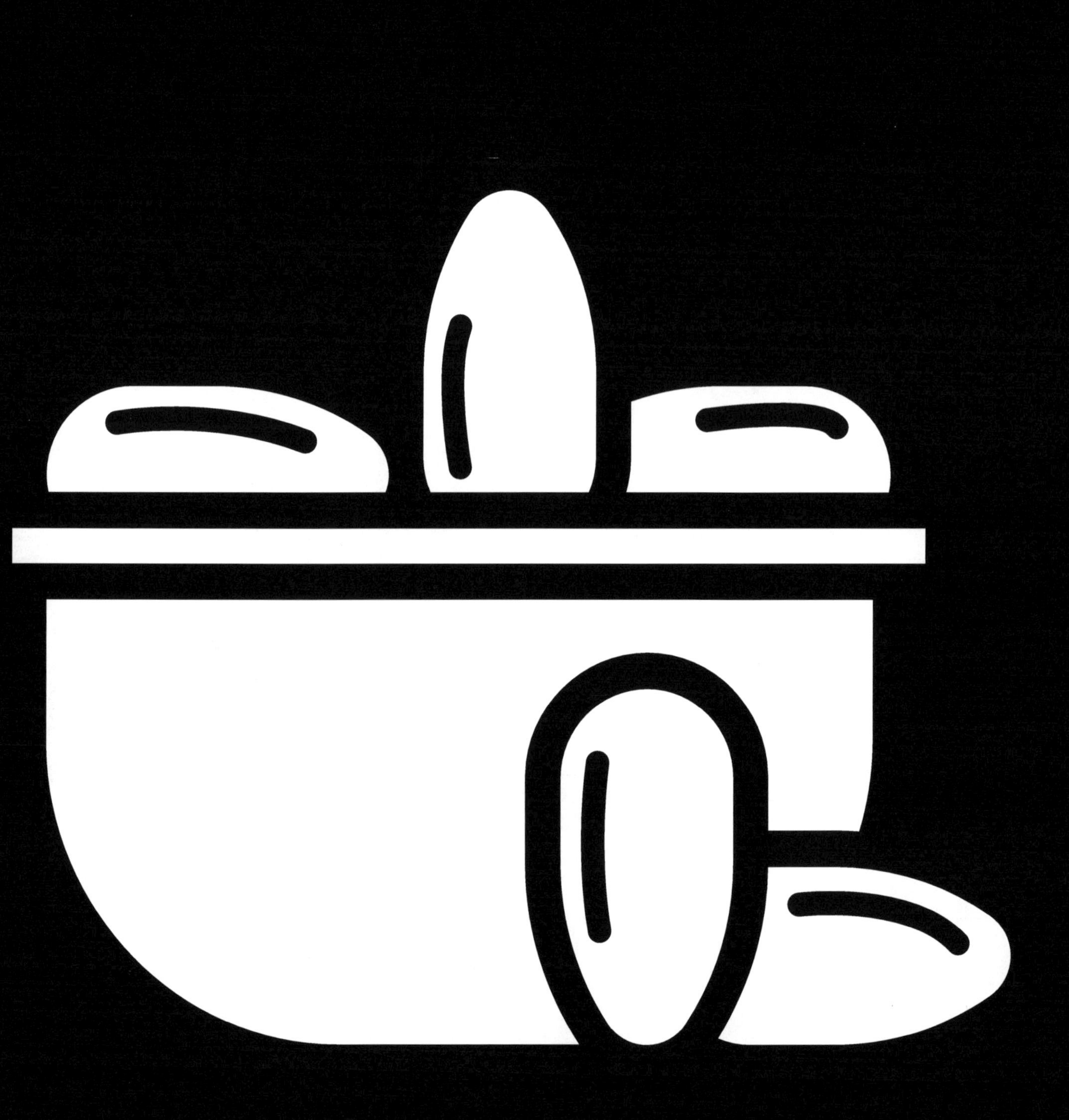

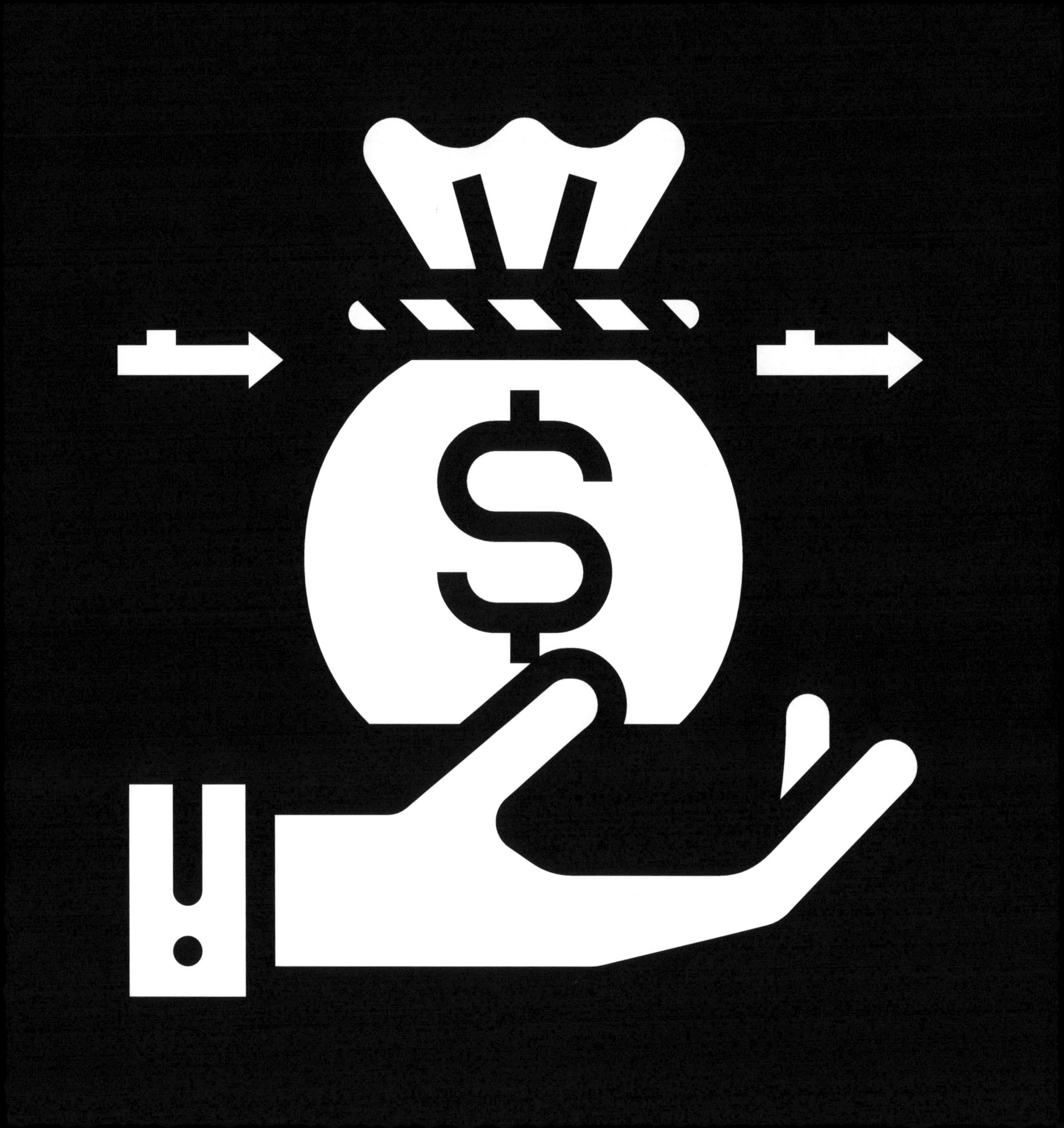

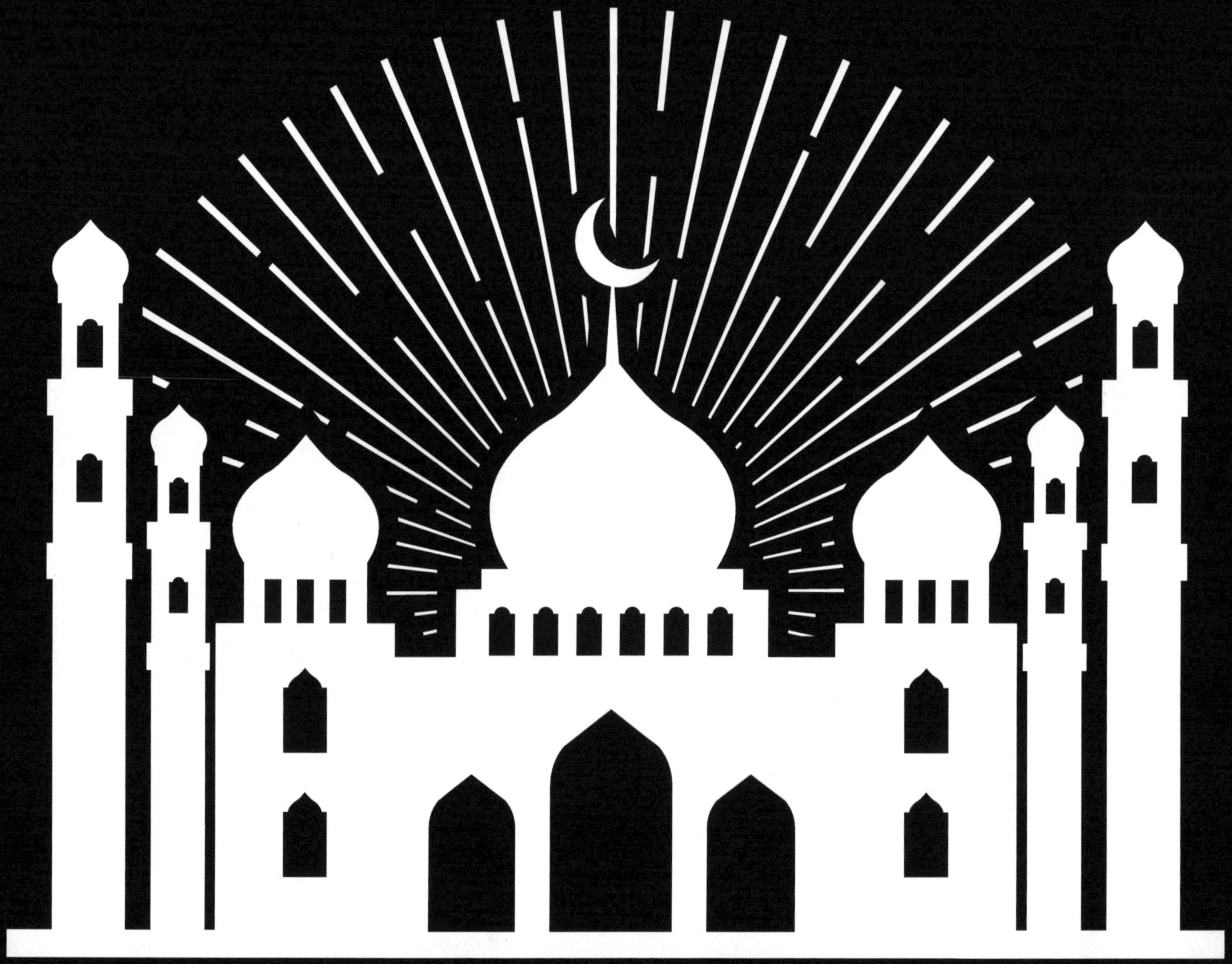

Made in the USA
Columbia, SC
16 March 2025